For an Hour, We Lived from Flowers

For an Hour, We Lived from Flowers

And Other Poems

Owi I. Nandi

iUniverse, Inc.
New York Lincoln Shanghai

For an Hour, We Lived from Flowers
And Other Poems

Copyright © 2005 by Abhijit Nandi

iUniverse books may be ordered through booksellers or by contacting:

iUniverse
2021 Pine Lake Road, Suite 100
Lincoln, NE 68512
www.iuniverse.com
1-800-Authors (1-800-288-4677)

ISBN: 0-595-33326-5 (pbk)

ISBN: 0-595-66844-5 (cloth)

Printed in the United States of America

Contents

Introduction

❦ "Lyrics, even if modern, should sing about those rare feelings that make up the salt of life, that make this path on earth unique..." states Owi Nandi, who would like to share these poems, which he originally published in German, with the English-speaking public. Each piece of Nandi's artwork is set in a silent moment, mostly written after his marriage in 1995 to his love, Annette. Yet the ideas for these lyrics have been collected since his late childhood. Nandi likes to illuminate the uniqueness of creation, and he also adores awakening the senses to the beauty of love and friendship. He has been inspired by many sources, from the simple words of people close to him to German, English, Greek, Arabic, Russian, Chinese or Indian poets. The author believes in the words of Jesus, and these words shine through in this book. Nandi also greatly values the insights from other philosophies and religions.

One of the common threads in Nandi's lyrics is the transience of time, which makes every moment in life so very precious. This may also be one of the reasons why readers of every age and origin find a part of themselves in his poems, and some readers would put these poems as a part of their daily meditations.

The author cherishes the free verse of today's lyrics and has chosen to write a variety of lyric and prosaic texts. He plays with line and poem length, punctuation and its absence, and the complexity and simplicities of language.

The author would like to thank Timothy Peter Colman (originally from England, living in Switzerland) for his most valuable suggestions for translating these German poems. Chloé Galley (UK), Nandadulal Nandi (India), Merran Matthews (Australia), Christopher Hardy (US), Millie Sealana de Quiroga (US), Sara Crockett (US), Shea Spindler (US) and the reviewer from iUniverse.com for their help in correcting English words and grammar. Thanks are also due to Nandi's friend Thomas, a passionate nature photographer, for his poetic pictures. Read more on Nandi and his friends on www.gedichte.tv.

We lived

For an hour we lived from peonies
flowers freighted with pollen
this day in May
without holding hands

I wanted to ask you
to explain to me
the meaning of friendship
and we esteemed it
beyond all borders

Now again, they flower
only for a short time
freighted with pollen
in a bottomless deep
red

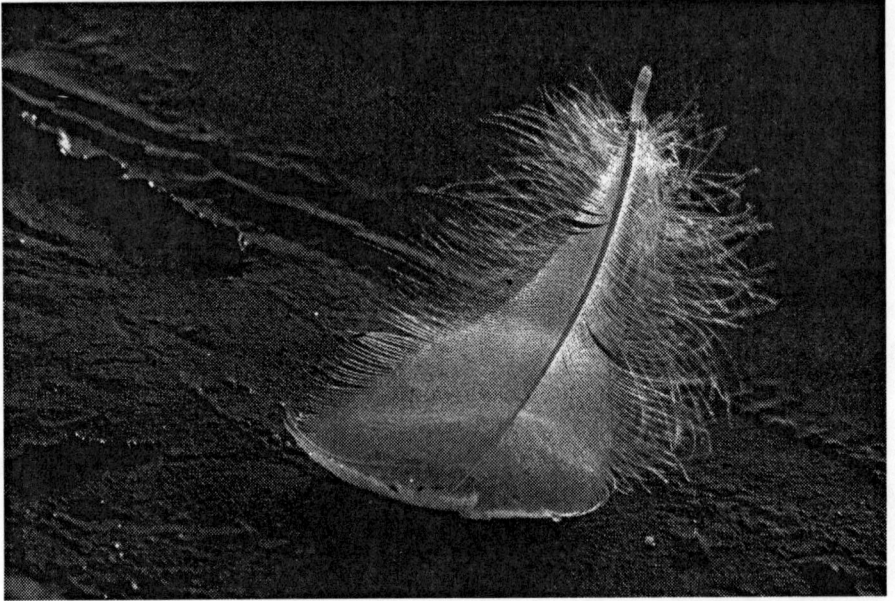

Summer on a lake

The down of the swan's bow dances waxen
on the soft water surface,
indulges in ease,
unable to think of the next tempest.

Emerald dragonflies carve jags into the cheesy air,
twitching into the small inlets,
whirring on the spot during the next breath.
Their copper-colored abdomen is laced up
like the waistline of a female motorcyclist
wrapped in leather.

The corpses of last and distant years' leaves
rest on the lake's muddy floor,
lost in growing old, blacking on,
bordered by dusky beechnuts.

The water sprinkles upon the cheeks,
plays and washes against its swimmers,
around the rush stalks ascending
over—slenderly from the depth
and the precious butter balls
of the flowering nuphars.

There were questions

There were questions which nobody
answered for you
Perhaps you merely resembled
a leaf
toy of the wind
too meaningless
on this scenery

Perhaps nobody wanted
to warm you up
nobody to exert justice
and still
the pansies
flower for you

Autobiography of a grasshopper

I sang all my life long
and fell silent
when it got colder.

Obituary for the same grasshopper

He spent an inconspicuous
and happy childhood
as a larva,
rejoiced at the summer,
attended with great care
to his duty of finding a partner.
Above all, let us mention
that he sang untiringly.
Autumn had to signify his death.

Spoken images while falling asleep

Over vitreous hills grabs the snow,
and from the tottering gravestones
the cats creep, feigning grief.

Rumbling in the underground
where the worms miss
the feeling of time
—unfortunately.

The gleaming moon
covers the fallow grounds.
The extinct Little Owl
claws at a mouse
and flies away noiselessly
into the night.

In the bones of the earth
sleeps the day or
hunts forgetfulness.
Root meshes pervade the shelter.

I know you for sure, Andreas
—I met you yesterday:
Out of the undertow of subconsciousness
batters the meaningless
like the droplet atop the water
that swallows it.

A nightly fountain

The precious hours
of loving couples
flow by at the nightly fountain.
Arrogantly, without being asked,
the endless water arc
plunges out of the tube
to be collected
in the old, red sandstone basin.

The beautiful hours of the living
flow by
at the nightly fountain.
The octagon only dams up
the most recent, lucid past.

The waiting hours of the homeless
flow by
at the nightly fountain,
frozen and undisjointed.
Countlessly,
their heartbeats are shed.

Transitoriness of the Dawn

How old had I to be,
to hope that everything
would always become better?
How old to ask,
where the clouds come from?

When was it, when you,
for the first time,
were embraced by love?
When had you not yet
realized
that life can be hard?

We confined ourselves
to these questions:
Out of respect
for the transitoriness
of the Dawn.

The poesy

The poesy of the beginning
of a poem or a novel
often resides in the fact
that the composition sets in,
as if it were cut out of full life,
out of the banality, the banal,
unadorned simplicity.

Polyphony

Perhaps you could compare
human cultural history
with a polyphonous piece of music,
in which Technology, Society, Politics,
Music, Science, Painting, Philosophy,
Literature, and Religion
evolve as independent voices,
but not without mutual adaptation.

Confessions

These days, hardly anybody
goes to confession any more.
Confessions happen
in the admission conversations
of devoted homeopaths, today.

Snow flurry

Out of the white sea of the soils
and the white sky, spitting snow flakes,
the silhouettes loosen
like the names
of Bernese farmsteads,
naking alders,
linden trees
and of a forest
from the nearby horizon.

On the first ice day

On the first ice day,
I was seeking
a virtually
objective definition
of friendship
and had to give the answer
to myself.
So thin was the ice.

Trace of two lifetimes

On the special request of his most faithful user, a computer drew a dibiogram, such is the technical term—the trace of two lifetimes.

In the beginning, René was blue, and Anita was green. The colors were similar somehow, by chance.

Both lines began nearly on the same height—they were born in the same year.

The course of the two traces indicated how near to each other Anita and René had come during different times in their lives. Almost endlessly, the lines swung away from each other and towards each other again, without ever touching. On page 103, both of them were 27—the two lines happen to near each other by a hair's breadth (encounter in the train to Berne, talk about the next elections). No—no beginning of a friendship, no falling in love, on either side. The two would not have remembered each other after ten years.

Several more times their paths crossed, without them taking notice of one another.

One trace ended earlier.

And humans (1996)

And humans grow up
in great freedom,
to argue with each other:
Christians against Christians,
to be happy about one another:
others about others and different looking ones.

And all of them go their ways,
some alone, others together
and yet alone, and still others together,
and perhaps without the feeling
of being alone.

And are already growing old by the age of eight,
then again at thirty and
possibly many times over,
accuse pessimism,
accuse submissiveness,
and still hope as grey-haired children.

Sins of omission

Under certain conditions,
an unwept tear,
a pellet of an owl not pulled into pieces,
an unsmelled book odor,
an untaken walk,
a nap not indulged in,
an unprolonged friendship,
a ripe question not asked.

Yearning

She had to bid farewell to Earth
and would have given everything
to come back once again to this place;

it was not to have been her homeland.
The sight of a curbstone of a sidewalk,
dirty from the abrasion of car tires,
would already have made her unspeakably happy.
Also, the sight of a tree, merely the vision
of a heron, a rat, of a breaking wave,
of a human being, of her love.

On the day before a night

On the day before a night
a bird slept a dream
and I froze…
that a bird can dream.

Diary entry

In his letter, he apologized once more
for his parting, which was so prompt;
the window pane would have already
separated them one from another.

The three-and-a-half hours
would have been used up so quickly;
he would gladly have
looked after her for longer,
but the quick good-bye
would be the most approved.

She had not thought so far,
did not turn back either,
or attach the same esteem
to the three-and-a-half hours.

In his diary, he secretly recorded the
three-and-a-half hours,
in the evening,
in broken Russian,
so that nobody would be able to read it.

Skeleton of a candle

Skeleton of a candle,
gnawed away under the
watchful eyes
of the mother of God.

The bit of warmth
resounded
in the masonry.
Wishes still hover here,
for the new year,
which is going off outdoors.

The question of sense

The question of sense, as such,
should not be viewed
as detached
from the belief in love.

Churches

Romanic churches
as your
maternal
grandmother.
Tuffaceous limestone
you know.

Silent happiness

Often, in hindsight,
within the suffering,
lays the silent happiness.
Within the troubles,
the information achieved.

Three cursory questions, not to be taken too seriously

Are we the product of our genetic code
that grew up, was "cooked,"
in different regions of the world
during an unimaginably long history?
Are we the product of our senses
and the reason which is tied to them,
in a way, the victims of our readings,
acquaintances and experiences?
Are we presents of uniqueness and life?

Trial run in philosophizing

Nothing is thinkable without everything else.

Rowing

Rowing, the spring alienated,
muskrats gnawed at the digs.
Plywood piled up.
I bid you to come
and waited for
what would become of the freedom
that, by nature, lay ahead of us,
hoped not to become
what is called a Realist.

Perspective

Most poems
tell us about
Her, Him,
You, Me, or Us.
You confine yourself, humbly.
For the sake of simplicity.

Farewell

Today, she

sold her

weaver's loom.

Her eyes

have become

weak.

-

Severity of life—

in the welfare state.

Charnel-house

Silent singing of the ones
remembering the forefathers
in front of the hollow lindens,
the pestilence trees, charnel-houses
and abandoned barns
without peaceful churchyards.

Even the speechless rowed-up ones
do not count the cavern drops,
tame the bygone,
pay their tunes
in non-language.

Kriti

This odor was loaded with the memories
of oleander nights on Crete.
Faraway remembrances of a land in the sea,
bathed in the waves.
Memories, almost no longer true,
of moaning donkeys,
country women on the cucumber fields,
highly pregnant watermelons,
perspiring faces.
Theodorakis' music in the
bumpy, dust-bathed bus.

The disused windmills
and a soil, with which one could grow old,
like the mole.
The melody of the tiny fish while snorkling,
lemon—and olive-bosks on the Minoic red soil.
Tree frogs in the water tanks,
the heat, rehashed a thousand times
in the chirping of the cicadas.
A lot of rough salt of the sea,
the remembrance of a farewell
with a white towel and a few tears
in the heart.

Wrongfully—to May

You ask yourself rightly,
if it be allowed,
to write a poem
to May, today.

Offended by the sun
melted away,
root treated,
poured out the flowers.

To beloved May,
stress bathed:
You might be asking,
if the last
still counts as much.

Delphi

In the hills near Delphi
the scarabaeus beetles
certainly labour again,
with their dungpills.

Orchids miniatures,
Ophrys species,
delight in beauty
between the glistening limestone.

Mules
rest in the shadow, perhaps.
Wondering if Apollon still speaks
through riddling oracles.

Weight comparison

How much does a summer weigh?
A tear. A gram of salt on the skin.
A peach. A sour apple. A heavy wine grape.

How much does a life weigh?
Ten mourners. 70 kilograms.
A passion. An opus. A love.

And you go on ambling

And you go on ambling
by the villages and hostels
and hope again
for humans,
who do not give you.
Stones when bread was asked,
and you still hope
that there is something,
and that somebody pays you,
in case you fall among robbers.

This evening

This evening in the coldness of a third February
in the midnineties,
when we crossed the platanus avenue,
where in the spring the goldfinches natter,
I asked myself where are they now.
I mean: in the night…

Nightmare

Nothingness often disguised itself to the child
as a grid enfolded by blackness—
falling as a barrel, undulating, surrounding,
and robbing.

To cry out, consciousness was insufficient.

Anarchy

Les mouettes, the gulls, have no god,
he alleged,
and are anarchic,
upon which I would not be provoked.

Eyes to see, ears to hear

Then and when,
life knocks at me, knocks at the door,
and wants to make me believe.

It lets me feel my body, in my lifetime,
a river on its journey,
always further away
from the playful brook.

Then, I conquer back my augustness,
the youth, the faith.
I see and hear—
in silence and darkness, too.

How are the trees bent by the wind?

How are the trees bent by the wind?
Explain it to the one who has not seen it.

How does the water push
to form grey rings
on the brown river?
Explain it to the one who has not seen it.

How does an injured cat wail?
Explain it to the one who has not heard it.

How does a barley field smell at the end of May?
Explain it to the one who has never lived.

Computer code

```
Sub AnySub (love)
Dim love as Variant
Set love = 2
On Error Goto EndOfFile
return
```

In the Austrian Weinviertel

Wilderness ends the tamed land,
at the edge of the village,
at least, you can still imagine that.
That here, the geese grazed,
and on the open meadows,
the tiny plantlets at the village edge,
filled the places,
which now have become so rare.

Report from the winter woods

Fog nestles between trees,
the day only half breaks.
The snow underfoot,
dwindles in scrunching carpets,
sealed with the washed out traces
of large and small dogs,
of the fox lacings
and the tiny squirrel feet
as a joke motif.
At the hollowed trivium,
one catches the whiff
of the polecats fugitive stench, perhaps.
Fairy tale animals tease with betraying traces
and with certainty,
do not show their faces.

On Thursday

On Thursday I asked you
about your thoughts on Freedom.

On a Sunday,
how life would be after death.
You said you were Taoist,
and nobody has yet come back:

and since then I ask myself
what it means to grow older.

Homage to a life

Hommage à une vie
envie de penser
d'amour du paysage
amour
de passage
sans perdre
ses couleurs
hommage aux homards
et aux hommes
morts ou mortels
sans perdre l'idée
des printemps

Homage to a life
desire to think
of love for the landscape
love
of passing by
without losing
its colors
Homage to lobsters
man
dead or mortal
without losing the idea
of springtimes

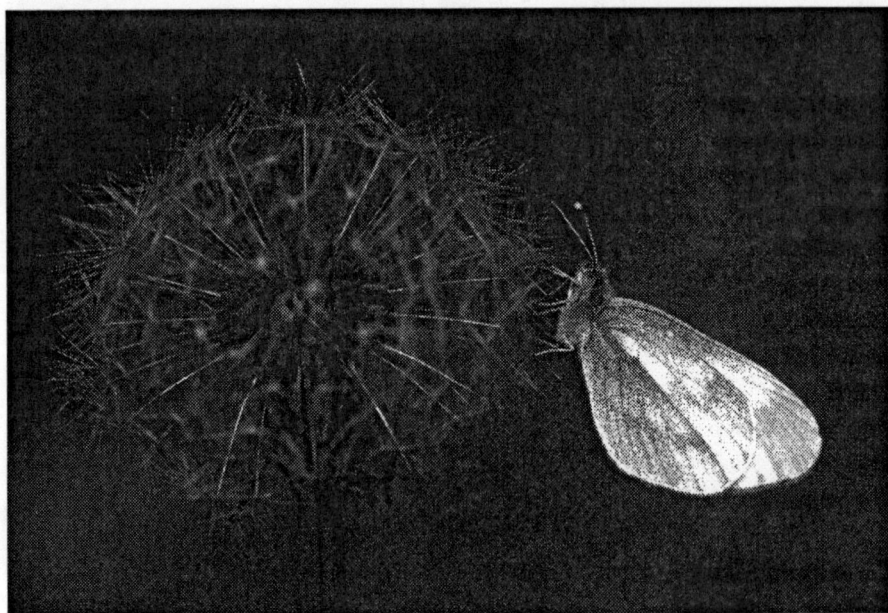

Wish for myself

Wish me
three wishes
one of which
as a path companion
Wish
a belief so deep
that it can move
mountains

She

She painted with words, droned with dishes,
wove in her dreams, knitted relationships,
caressed with her mind,
baked stones, savoured and smelled the wine's bouquet,
felt the violets,
sensed the brook, groped for music,
but remembered lovingly.

Deceased father in the dream of a dream

In the dream, he once more ascended
the mountain ridges with his father,
over the meads, where the marmots
no longer squeaked,
through furrows and trenches
and incisions
and by higher rock towers,
where the chamois droppings
lay scattered at their feet.

With his deceased father,
he once more climbed up
by the roaring brooks,
scoured the dense alpine shrubs,
where one could not gather berries any longer,
to a peak, where the choughs
screeched so penetratingly, in the summer,
and paddled with their tails and wings
around the ridges.

They wanted to see
if up there,
there already lay snow.

We lay down

We lay down
the program
of our let us say
friendship
within an hour
or let us say
it was
laid down

Bound to earth, earthlike

Earth, to me, is expressed by
a piece of neglected soil
between asphalt and walls,
a piece of ground with a handful
of indestructible weeds,
with a small and not straight path,
trampled out,
which follows a train track,
all astray, a couple of paper rags,
which no one uses anymore.

One would hardly find
such an island of earth
in Switzerland,
in such a narrowly circumscribed way,
yet, frequently, in Poland or India,
and certainly in other places, as well.

A piece of fiction exobiology

Let's assume a future being, endowed with intelligence, reaches the Earth and unravels a fossilized CD in the petrous strata of a well-preserved human city. With technological skills, this being discovers that information has been stored on this strange product, which codes acoustic waves. Assume further, this being is successful in reading this peculiar information, and in deciphering it into a document of sounds.

Apparently, this CD bore a sound work of humans from the period when computers were used. Further CDs are found by our extraterrestrial being and complete his picture about those interesting dwellers of the planet Earth. A science about human music is established. Would the being again assign an exceptional rank to a Beethoven piano concert? Would the being recognize some comforting and powerful feelings in this work of art, as well? Would the

being sense this music as artistic at all? Could it be impassioned by the most beautiful motif of the third phrase? Would it even be reminded of its own art? If the laws of physics are universally valid, would it be aesthetic of melodies, rhythms, and harmonies?

In the gleam of a torch

In the torch beam I asked myself
how narrow this way might be
how scantily measured out, so to speak

How far the beam would reach
why, this track which I laid
had an odor of melancholy

It was also
the fear of delirium
the feeling of loneliness
on the path
in nocturnal forest

Almost Winter

Sometimes snowflakes fall,
and paths turn white;
whereas, meadows remain green.

You are taken away
by the virginity of this whiteness,
like the voles, which over the night
pock up the fields with their crumbly heaps.

Dogs are being walked.
Tracks of skaters in fir-patterns
fly over the flat lanes,
and lone-wolf buzzards rest
on the field poles.

You are struck by houses with thick roofs;
older houses, simply built,
as they might have been impressed
in the imaginations of children,
and you are amazed:
they really exist.

The scenery is disguised now and then,
free of charge.

Salomé in a dream

Supressed murmuring in the hall.
Astray, on the floor,
ripped packages of potato chips.
Three rows of tables and chairs, slightly ascending
around the brightly lit scaffolding.
In a moment, the determined female dancer will enter.

The lights go out.
She enters.
A green spotlight strikes her in the midst
of the stage.
With arms outstretched, bending backwards,
she allows the applause to die away.
Nods are exchanged.

Her dark brown hair against the alabaster floor.
Golden earrings, hung with amber.
The lid-lines prolonged in black,
a proportionate, pretty face.
The shoulders naked,
a long gleaming dress
being neither light nor dark blue.

Her naked feet
bear little bells.
She dances.
Silence from the seats.
The naked feet violently tap over the floor.
Her blue dress flies.
The calves jerk in the light of the reflectors.
Her hair dances wildly across a face
and hides her features.

Suddenly, a crystal bowl slips out of her robe
and bursts with a loud noise
on the alabaster floor.

The light goes out.
Shock.
Whispering in the audience.

Question to an old man

"Now then, has everything that really
should have been said,
been said?"
A youngster might ask an old man.
"I don't think so, at least it had not been yesterday.
Would I have ever gone through puberty, otherwise?
Would I have ever told my parents,
not in this fashion, not in this well-worn way,
not by these established means, not by being so self-confident,
not by being so untruthful."
"In those days, did you still go through puberty?"
the youngster wanted to know from the old man.

Pagan springtime song

The flimsy cover of snow has sagged away.
The tiny, orderly braced disks of flakes
clot into vitreous grains.
And mighty raindrops clear up
the matted remains of winter's dress.

Flora and Faun wake up from endless dreams.
The first one, extraneous and feeding,
slinks into twigs and buds,
into roots and tubers, announces warmer days.
Suspiciously she glances to the sky,
wanting to receive clear and strong light.

Faun awakes—restlessness welling and begetting,
tickles the stiff wings and legs,
makes quiver and tremble, crawl, skip, or fly,
attacks its sleepy drove
with lust for rambling and mating.
His victims have to please,
singing, wooing, building, feeding.

Two daisy heads

Two daisy heads
she squeezed from their stalks,
meditated forgetfully about their shape,
and sacrificed them
to the innocence of the moment.

Blue robe with red and yellow spots

She built a blue house
and adorned it with scorching roses,
which were quicker to wither than her hopes.

Looked out of the window,
as if she could fly,
on her tender hands.

Over meadows of dandelions.

Love and death

Love and death devour the pages,
springtime and transience
and woe of being-no-more.

The longing to remain oneself,
to stand in the glare of happiness,
as I and You (or I with You)
and not to be talked out
of trembling and breathing so soon.

Aurora

The lotus-coloured aurora
on the way to work.
In the transience between providence
and mere coincidence.

At the age of thirty

At the age of thirty,
he claimed
that amorousness
arises from the joy
of striving for truth.

My dear moon

Good night
my dear moon
my dear

For consolation
I tie you down
to my bedspread
and let the sheen
of your glow
enfold my pale face

Between youth and old age

When I was small, lying in my bed,
the blanket pulled up to my neck,
at my grandmother's in the city,
I pictured, how I would awake as a grown-up.
One day in the morning,
hair on my legs and chest,
a deep voice, a large body, the same body.
That's how I am now.

—Recently, I walked over large granite boulders,
through a curtain of plants,
a little tired, a little shaky.
I pictured how I would walk some day,
with elderly skin on my legs,
the hairs on my chest white,
every step a gift.

Poem with the beginning of a pop song

Early in the morning
when people
dream about each other
early in the morning
when the white gulls
glide inaudibly
through the empty streets,
she wanders along lonesomely.

Frosting from the emptiness and chill
of the morning,
and the streetlamps dim
as if on command.
A new sun slice trundles over
the hairline of the horizon,
dazzles its orange refinery
into the chill.

Over the artfully sober pillars
of the railway poles,
a misty sky unravels its veil.
Her stomach craves
something warm.

Morning scene on Chalkidikí

In the early morning—
the light seeks the land
you love.

Over the old, curved earth line—
clarity gropes its way
and dogs bark—
dogs nobody calls by name.
Grass reeds—weighed down
with sleeping insects—
tremble in the cool breeze
that blows from the sea.
A cock crows—of course.
The shrubs grow out
of the darkness.

From the preceding orient—
a country greets
with the lively zeal
of an awakened day.

Stamps

"Yannis, my friend,
are you still enthusiastic
about the amphibians in the pond?"
"Micha, when I am sad,
I get drunk
with Greek music.
I turn on the dance-floor
like a child."
"Yannis, do you still remember the stamps?"
Those, we swapped
on Wednesday afternoons?
Carefully preserved ones,
with images that caught our fancy.
Yannis, my friend,
do you still refuse
to ever become an adult?"

Wideness

Over gentle coastal knolls we strolled
in the midst of an English summer,
accompanied by the turquoise-colored sea,
with its soft waves dashing against the rocks
far below the steeply breaking edge of the land.

Big white gulls drew their loops slightly off the shore
and now and then nasally screeched.
We could have wandered endlessly
through pastures covered in short grasses,
interspersed by minute blossoms.

Rarely grew a shrub.
The paths, barely two feet wide,
ran narrowly through the meadows
and glanced at us in tender loam-colored tones.
The sunlight flew slightly, turbidly,
but in a summerly evereness
through the pale, greyish-blue sky.

We breathed the wideness and gentleness of the scenery.

Autumn flower

I will surrender to the snow,
will let myself be covered,
when the sun lowers,
when bitterness will reign,
will not speak,
as my year is over.

What remained

The funeral oration
remained objective,
though his life
had not always
been so.

The row of numbers
broke off at some point in time.
It tore apart under
its own weight.

What remained
were these boxes.
What remained
was the perished memory,
not even
the melancholy.

W.C.

A place to be lost in thoughts,
a place to indulge
in the pattern-loving
subconscious.

The sight, mostly directed downwards,
no distraction.
Just take the tiles on the floor!
Some of them can be grouped
into crosses.

You can measure small tiles
against the large ones,
your eyes can combine
large squares, starting from small ones.
Darker and lighter shades of colors
alternate and form figures.
Silverfish flit into the tiny cracks.

Presummer

Before summertime
the black redstart atop the chimney
grinds his song
into the mild evening air

The bones of the dead tree
blaze in the fire
The cuckoo chortles its name
while the twilight
hesitatingly sets in

The ants look
for their simple path
on the red currant bush
and the remains of the fire
surrender
ashen-grey
before summertime

Seals

You gracious playful faces of the sea,
creatures immersed in love,
with round bald-pated heads and dark knob-eyes,
neckless with a cat's snout.
Dogs and people of the sea
with vigorous cone-shaped bodies,
four limbs spread into fins,
the belly formed as a large, caterpillar underside.

When I first discovered you,
aged five, in the animal park,
between the whiffing pine martens
and the dusky raccoon dogs,
you grew into my soul and advanced into my dreams.
Your curiously nodding heads before feeding,
nimble as the one of an Indian dancing girl.

This crawling on land, the troubles,
which you accept to be free in water.
This rolling in the midst of a full-diving run,
and this slipping onto the next shore.
Everything entertained me
and stimulated my curiosity.

You playful brethren of the sea:
Will there still be a place in our hearts for you
in the times ahead?

Secret evolution

Secrets
are passed
through generations
or eventually
they are lost

Vie *

He was almost twenty years old when he went to France for the first time along with his friend. First, to the Camargue, which left its impressions indelibly written into their books of life. Then, to the neighbouring Crau, that peculiar provencial desert of pebble stones, where they listened to the whistles of the thick-knee, where they came across the fragile flowers of the deep red adonis and where he found a stone, a flat limestone, which you might have slated across the water. On this stone you could read clearly—as if by chance—the capital letters *V I E*. Soon after, he lost this stone again.

French for "life"

Three impressions between conscious thinking

The soft midland lake becomes an amniotic sac to her
for the duration of an almost unconscious swim,
the floating over the blue water,
between hazy-blue mountains,
beneath a blue ending sky.

An excessively large shadow weighing zero grams
of a fine-membered foot,
eked out into the air,
falls onto the whitewashed wall.

A smell, better yet, a mix of smells
of something he cannot name,
perhaps cow dung, the steam of a gas lamp,
or loam soaked in fuel reaches his nose—uncalled for
and takes him back for a fraction of a moment
—to India

In this one moment

Happy
without punctuation marks
was I in this
one
moment in time
so much so
that I could not
rule out
timelessness

Iris

In the small, silty rivulet
along the railway dam
stood the first one
which I noticed consciously
The first Iris
with smooth, blade-like leaves.

Its shape settled down immediately
in my imagination
as if I had only
waited for this being.
I never saw it blossom
but its name did not let me go.
I dug it out and planted it
in my parents' garden
where it never flowered
only waiting for a day to die.

I saw Iris flowers
growing on meagre limestone
on the long slope above Delphi
on a Greek Easter day,
at the beginning of April,
in a short, pale-green meadow
with some junipers.

An enchanted couple on short stalks
with big, full flowers
in the midst of this barrenness.
The Attic Iris, perhaps,
one pale yellow
the other violet-brown.

A pair that complements
not far from the place
where I turned back the first day

without having seen
the snow-covered summit of Mount Parnassos.

I met them in hundreds
all together as picked holy flowers
at the feet of a risen Virgin Mary
during the Easter week in Seville.
Small blue Iris flowers,
with yellow marks in their gullets,
lined up to form a carpet beneath
a motionless statue
which was later carried through the crowd.

Nothingness

In the kernel of the fruit
rests embedded on
nothingness
the sleeping life
essence and rondelay
of tomorrow's sceneries
coming bukolis
wise greenswards orphans
of the present

Oedipus complex

The relationship of the
Oedipus complex
to progress
relies on the fact
that in each generation,
the sons think
that their fathers
could not have
conceived
what they themselves
do conceive.

It looks

Greece brought along
its islands herself.
The delphiniums, their blue
The Akropolis bore its *K,*
long before the ravages of time
could harm her.
Poseidon now dances with Orestes,
Aesculap has not died,
and Odysseus might
not yet have returned
from his sailings.

Flow me

Flow me   Flow me
You   You
stream me   just stream
or   through
along me   greens
close

                    You are

Green and blue   What else?
when the snow   Roses
on the flat soil   thorn-less ones.
with breathing ones   Sloes.
and no longer   Where we
                                        breathe.

Still?

Sometimes I wish to know

Sometimes I wish to know,
who would prove correct,
who would prove to have
acted or thought correctly,
then, when everything
dissolves,
when only
understanding and love prevail.

—If at all, anyone still could prove correct.

Who would prove correct:
those who fought incensedly
against the wear and tear of nature,
or those who made
the pleasure of life to their only content.

—If then, it would not be both or none.

Those who believed in fidelity,
in commandments,
or those who only made
their feelings their standard,
those assumed to be frail
or those who cared for them.

—If then at all, there could still be perceived.

Addendum to El Rocío

By the way
I could have mentioned
this resin odor
of the Cistus bushes

And the calls
of the bee eaters
which I could restore
in my memory
only with the help
of the videotape

The ant highway
on the worn path
in the patchy grass cover
The dog, which followed us

I could have mentioned
so much more
It continues
to grow older now
in my memory

A further impression of Venice

Venice, away from land, on tight space,
so much angulation, uncounted lanes,
in which you can get lost,
as before the time of maps.

Millions of preserved piles,
agreeably stinking broth
under the gondolas,
centuries of people
searching for romance.

Jewels from the wide world,
gathered by sea.
Fine art, which implants itself
into the halls.
At low tide, seaweeds
grasping to the lane flanges.

Fish, which are still sold
in the markets,
mushrooms and fresh food,
from the countryside that still exists,
a word against the opinion that
unspoiled entirety
is in a state of foundering.

Courting couples from around the world
and rags of words from the other people
in all the familiar sayings.
Chinese folksongs.

Three times

Past is filled with poesy
because it did not repeat

The present possesses the senses
which sense only now

For the future we hope
since we want to experience it
as worth living.

Springtime in the floodplains of Switzerland

Blue bells
Woodlets of spring
on the river
Floodplains
and heavy
bumble bees
in my
Springtime

Lemon colored butterflies
and some leaves of wake-robins
Catkins of willows
embracing
not kissing
And yet
Springtime

Much dampness still
from the textbooks
brown soils
and upon it
flocks of
merry lapwings

Green and red
bicycles
New-blue
windows (above)
and still
springtime

Penduline tits
on the outermost twigs
Odour of loam
I mean
springtime

The clear calls
of the tits
So much brightness
on these
walls
Your springtime

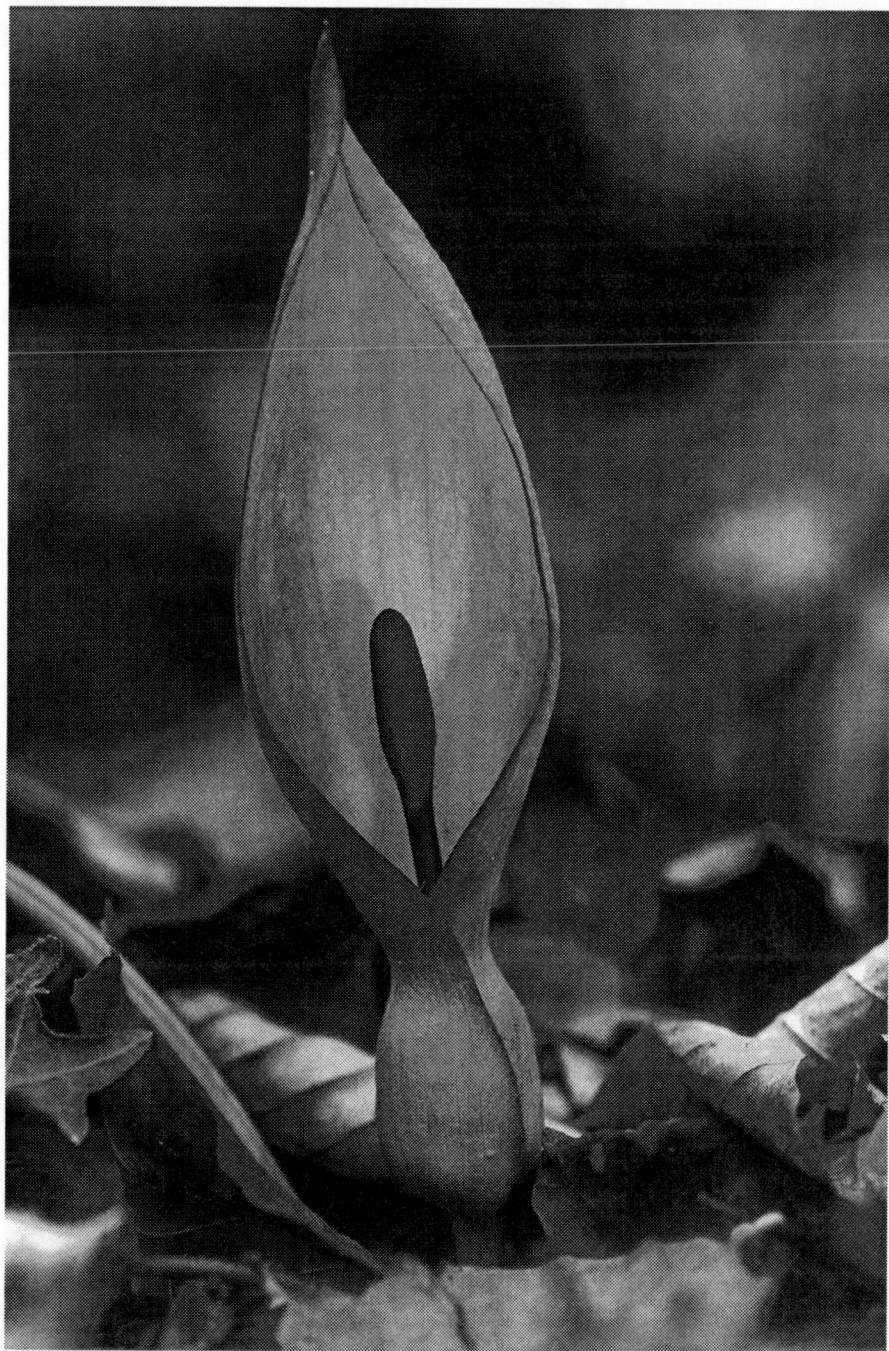

Impressions of a dream

And that's why I invented the rhyme
to build up something on it
in claustral arrest
Japanese
on the lake of Brienz
where the big fish emerged
and made us friends
the last one of the group
In front of your wisdoms
we had to be awestruck
and also we had
to make new friends from old ones

Full moon in July

Full moon in July
for the relatives
of others
moreover
pale and cold
at the turning point
of the moon's cycle

Wait

Wait my love
wait with aging
Shouldn't we prefer
to enjoy the dew drops
of the pre-summer

Wait and if you have
not yet tried
all the recipes

I am still able
to count all our years

Only twice
bloomed the lawn
in front of your parents
purple-colored house

Love

Some may say
Love is dead today
Some may say
Love may not die

Mourning labor

They said
mourning labor
and meant
labor

generous
on both ends
jetsam of a
       yet
unexplored ocean

it seems
out of decision
or mere chance

Give me once more

Once more
give me
your hand
as it was

Once more
give me
your words
about the warmth
during the cold
season

Once more
give me
this
blue-goldened
gift wrap paper
at which
I rejoiced
like an king

Yi Guo Tang

Yi guo
A bowl of
Tang
Soup
(noodle soup).

Glossary

Rushstalk: the long stalk of a slender water or marsh plant

Nuphars: yellow water lilies

Bernese farmsteads: the beautiful old farming houses in a region of central Switzerland

Alder: a broad-leaved tree of temperate climate zones

Pellet: a regurgitated, elongated structure of hairs and bones that can not be digested by an owl

Romanic: a style of church architecture in Europe from the 11th and twelfth century AD

Muskrat: a large rodent, similar to a beaver but without a flattened tail

Minoic: the earliest period of Cretan civilization

Ophrys: small, handsome orchids imitating the bodies of various insects

Trivium: bifurcation of a path

Polecat: a species of the family of martens; they are rather small carnivorous mammals

Chamois: a hoofed alpine animal with crooked horns

Choughs: black alpine crow birds with yellow bills

Daisies: small composite flowers with tiny white rays and yellow center, typical for meadows in temperate Europe

Chalkidiki: three-fingered peninsula in the North of Greece

Redstart: a bird species with a red tail

Camargue: the delta of the Rhône River in France, a marshland with thousands of birds and white horses

Provence: a Mediterranean region in Southern France

Crau: a pebble-stone desert to the East of the Camargue

Thick-knee: a bird that is marvellously camouflaged in dry, stony environments

Adonis: a beautiful, deep red flower of unfertilized soils

Seville: an old city in Andalusia, southern Spain

Bukolis: lovely landscape with meadows and trees as conceived in Greek Mythology

Sloes: a European shrub flowering in early spring and bearing small, blue fruits in autumn

El Rocío: small village in the Coto Doñana National Park in Southern Spain; the Gypsies go on a pilgrimage to its famous church every year from all over the country.

Cistus: a Mediterranean shrub with flowers somewhat reminiscent of roses.

Bee eater: one of the most beautifully coloured European birds, nesting on sunny, sandy slopes and eating bees and other larger insects.

Wake-robin: a herbaceous plant of the Araceae family flowering in early spring

Lapwing: a funny, hooded bird-genus of the Northern Hemisphere

Penduline tit: a small bird species constructing hairy, overtopped nests

Yi Guo Tang: Chinese for "a bowl of soup"

Annette Nandi

Annette and Owi married in 1995. She works as a kindergarten teacher in the canton of Aargau, Switzerland. Annette has a great love for animals, her special darlings including geckos, seals, dolphins, baby gorillas, and even very small and inconspicuous creatures. She also likes painting and drawing. Her favorite themes are water surfaces, the interfaces between air and water, iridescent colors, and flowers, such as the poppies on the cover of this book, which she painted many years ago. Annette has a good taste for wines and cooking. She cooks with great passion, combining the healthy essence of nature's gifts with delicate taste. She receives inspirations from all over the world, including Japan (sushi), China (tofu dishes), Thailand (Thai curries), India (Bengali dishes which she learned from Owi's father), Bolivia (ají de gallina), USA (brownies), Italy (pasta all aglio e oglio), France (dishes from Burgundy) and the Canary Islands (papas con mojo). She especially likes to cook for friends. Annette cherishes her memories of her travels to South America and to Mongolia. Her favorite music is salsa, merengue and traditional Mongolian music.

Annette, together with Owi and Joacim, in a banana plantation on the Canary islands

The author

Owi Nandi, son of an Indian father and a Swiss mother, was born in 1966 in Wettingen, Switzerland. He discovered his great love for nature and philosophy early, which continually shines through in his written work. The author is married to Annette Nandi, a kindergarten teacher with great passion for drawing. Owi Nandi studied botany, zoology, and bio-mathematics in Zurich. In 1997, he completed his doctorate at the Philosophical Faculty of the University of Zurich (his PhD included a comprehensive morpho-logical analysis of flowering plants under the inclusion of molecular biological data, published in renowned journals of botanical science). Owi pursued his stud-ies in phytochemistry, land plant phylogeny, and pharmacology. Together with nature photographer Thomas Marent, he has authored many scientific and popu-lar articles. Owi Nandi was awarded with a lyric award of the National Library of the German Poem (Nationalbibliothek des Deutschsprachigen Gedichtes) in 1998. He ranked within the final winners in several contests on the Internet, such as in leserkreis.de, niederngasse.com, poetry.com, Noblehouse Publishers and voicesnet.org. Owi's English poems will be printed in early 2005 with an Ameri-can publisher.

Hobbies of the author include: ornithology, Chinese medical herbs, traveling, linguistics, and Greek music. The author is currently working as a scientific expert in the field of systematic identification and toxicology of Chinese and Indian medicinal herbs with a renowned small Swiss company. Owi is also inter-ested in dancing, healthy cooking, wines, human evolution, philosophy, and medicine.

For more on the author and his publications please consult: www.owi-nandi.com and www.gedichte.tv/english.htm.

The author sitting below a Gunnera–plant in the Botanical Garden of Kew, London.

0-595-33326-5

LaVergne, TN USA
10 August 2010
192773LV00002B/1/A